Kiss the Earth

Images & Words
Neal Sehgal

ISBN: 0-692-07985-8
ISBN-13: 978-0-692-07985-0

this is for the lost ones.
if you are reading this,
then we have found each other.
and now we can traverse
the bewildering wilderness
of this universe together.

there arrives a time
when you will begin again
from the beginning
for the very last time.
it is a thunder born from the quiet.

          you will hear it when it comes.

truth
needs no audience
nor applause.
it stands alone,
complete unto itself.
a star on its own stage.
a star in its own sky.

mighty bird,
fly higher.
hold on to the ether
with the grasp in the flap of your wings
and do not turn back around.
those who have conquered gravity
have no call to return to the ground.

this work–
        is it not worship?
this world–
        is it not my temple?

escape inside your soul.
there is a paradise of dreams
praying to be discovered,
hoping you will remember
all that you have lived,
so that you can tell the others–
still asleep far before the gate's end–
when you awake amongst the awakened.

to value living more than one's life...
the irony.
the paradox.
the curse.
the blessing.
parables of melancholy are scribed from here.
an infinite and enduring draw of lessons
repeating themselves—
the greatest stories ever told.

i wish i knew you
when your wave crashed upon the shore,
so i could be the drift of sand
that you secured into the sea evermore.

the beach's breeze brought to me
hints from the brush of her hair.
and when i breathed her in,
i forever forgot the taste of air.

as she walked along the shore,
her legs scribbled proverbs in the sand.
a mantra of vowels purred from the waters
as she greeted the waves with the touch of her hand.

this i witnessed from afar—
her warmth that shamed the summer.
and now that my senses are seized by her,
i may never really experience another.

i passed through them all,
mistaking each mirage as my future
but it was you all along—
an avatar not yet incarnated—
with each past nothing more than a
prelude to the here:

                      you.

shoulder to shoulder,
with their lattice of fingers laced like a tether
and their eyes affixed toward the planetary figure,
they knew the distance was not to dread but to discover
because no matter what destiny had to offer,
they would eternally journey in this world together.

men forget
        that as boys they once danced in the dirt and
women remind
        the days when they imbued their faces in it,
        together laughing in the breeze,
        one breath short of breathless…

he sang in shapes
and she listened in colors,
tapping to the beat of the algorithm
on each other's knees.
it was the music they made,
the dance in their dalliance.

"kiss me," said the sky.

ignite.
set flame to fire.
burn to ash those torrid memories.

extinguish.
rain down the tears of love lost.
breathe a new life to live.

emerge from it all like the phoenix
and raise your empire to lofty clouds
that only you can reach.

on those late summer evenings—
heavy and humid—
the sun does not set,
it spills softly
like watercolors
down a naked canvas.
and somewhere amidst
these traipsing hues
of purple and blue,
i spiral through to awaken at my center.
and in this mandala that i have become—
outstretched with gratitude—
enlaced with possibility—
i feel the long-awaited respite
of being entirely alone.

snow-winged bodies
s e p a r a t e
across the rippled waters
with dreams to reunite
around the purlieu
of their feathered necks.
these wings fly with wistful fervor,
ushered by the conspiring winds outré.
for those enamored by the eyes of another,
even tomorrow seems too far away.

just beyond our destiny,
high in the sky,

lies a greater dream still
that we can only awaken to
by laying rest to the past.

to get there,
we must let go of those
who have let go of us.

our hands must be as free as wings,
if we wish to fly.

breathe. believe. become.
and then
be
it
proudly
over
and
over
and
over
again

.

wrinkled foliage–
marked by time but beautiful.
ascend as you fall.

there is a story in our hands—
in who we have held
and how we let them go.

there is a story in our eyes—
in what we have seen
and for whom the tears we shed.

there is a story on our lips—
in who we have kissed
and the words we spoke to praise them.

there is a story in our hearts—
in all that it has felt
and the beating it took to love deeply.

our bodies are temples of the past—
an urn of fading memories
that honor our wrinkled skin and worn feet.

how can aging
be anything less than adorning
with a history like this.

it is difficult to remember
that lust for the divine
yields a fruit far sweeter
than that of the flesh.
but when tasted for a moment,
floods through my spine
like the whitewater of a rapid.
i find it in the absence of sound.
i find it in the heat of my hands
pressed against each other.
i find it in the leaves of trees,
and in the air that rustles between them.

you once spoke to me with a touch.
it was the most beautiful silence i ever heard.

there are a million ways
to express
adoration for another,
but none so true
as to utter,
"i believe in you."

...and as i look back on it all now, my dear,
the memories i choose to remember
are always written in cursive—
for the ways you took my breath away
made me forever more alive.

there is freedom in the loneliness.
there is adventure, too.
no one has yet charted the course
for you to find yourself back to you.

hate is not the tall tower of strength
that it tells itself to be.
it is the wreckage from a broken love
that longs to be whole again...
          with sobs that sound much like screams.

the waters are quiet now.
just me.
and the ripples that are made,
i made
and they
echo out to the periphery.

healing is this solitude.
infectious is this stillness.

experience infinity.
transcend your senses.
shatter the shackles
of consequences,
for those who truly live
never really die.

be the one fish who swims through the sky.

a cry morphed into a laugh
in a peculiar twist
of temporal felicity.
and the befuddled tears
which remained,
lamented the loss of their identity.

when we dance with abandon
and laugh ourselves into a cry,
when we are kind with none to witness
but allow none to do us wrong,
we honor the divine.

it was this light that gave us life,
and this light we are.
there is no greater worship
than to be humbly alive.

to separate the supernatural from the science,
we must ask "why?"
repeatedly with each row down the murmuring river
until we arrive at its mouth,
whose answer at last becomes
"i do not know."
and when you respond with a laugh so untamed
that it tickles even those beyond the brink,
it is only then you will know
that you have discerned
the tales we tell
from the truth untold.

i have died many deaths
only to awake again with each sunrise.
yet still so long it took me to learn
that permanence is nothing but a daydream.

and if i am to arise again to another morning,
let it be with gratitude.
i pray,
let it be with gratitude.

there is always a way.
what rock,
when under pressure,
is impermeable to the cunning of water?

i won every war i ever fought,
but never was there a victory
that was worth the casualties that it yielded.

what did i gain? not enough.
what did i lose? too much.

from an infinity of time lost, i came to learn
one does not need to fight every war
brought to their door.

the fire is burning warmly inside on those cold days.
seek its comfort with folded hands.
bar the gates, and do what they will not:
                    b   r   e   a   t   h   e.
             anger is death. forgiveness is life.

mediocre minds
will always spit malice in the face of your greatness.
marring the image of you
is far easier than reflecting
on the myriad of ways they
                failed themselves.

the moment you respond to a fool
is the very moment you too become one.

to grow,
to grow,
to grow its royal crown,
without thinking itself too triumphant for its throne.
that is the task that lays before the seed.

ego
sails across
a world of words
to stutter
what the stillness
of our own heart
sings
in
silence

.

each time a love is lost,
the less our heart will find in the next.
the more we give away,
the less we have left to give.
the heart is an organ of flesh,
but love is not.
                    still it is true–
too many beatings and it will cease to beat.
to the naive and the new,
there is more fervor to be found
in the friction of a few.

go on.
gaze into the eyes of another.
do you not see yourself reflected back in them?

just because we can,
does not mean we should,
and just because it has always been,
does not mean it should always be.
this world is ours to create.
we need only a vision
that transcends what we see.

whether we walk, crawl, slither, swim or fly...
we are one,
by breath and by blood,
in our desire to live and in our fear to die.

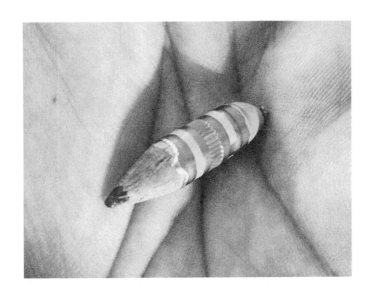

there is only one war worth fighting.
and within it,
ignorance is the enemy,
children are our army,
and classrooms are our battlefields.

these moments—
they are notes to a song
revealing themselves in reverse—
each a beginning to the end.
a melody to which only few care to listen.

embrace the yes,
accept the now,
dance to excess,
and
then take a bow.

you are deserving
of all the love that flows toward you,
and laced within it, drifts the duty
to break down the walls of your dam
and let the waters run free.

the fire of our anger does not burn bright forever.
inside our soul is a stream of relieving water
that slowly moves through us.
we must remember this when the heat of our lips
begins to spark its words.

when the river runs dry,
kneel down
and turn your tears
into rain.

everything a fire touches
too turns to fire.
set your soul ablaze
and allow it to inspire.
long after you are gone,
you will not only be remembered
for the embers
arising from the ashes,
but for the flames
untamed
that rage among the masses.

the great revolution of the world begins with you—
the moment you begin to live your life for yourself.

the sun stole away
the splendor of the other stars,
not by tucking them between
the folds of the night's sky,
but by shining brighter.

some sentences are the spawn of wounds.
to write them is to heal.
from these words, we will bleed.
in these words, we will breathe.

a crop circle has appeared on my field–
a mandala of geometry laid across stalks of wheat
i pressed in the night before retiring for the day.
i wanted to remind myself,
for when i awake,
that i too am made of magic.

the fireflies toast the night,
lauded by the empyrean,
swallowed by the shadow
from the sky of obsidian.

holy tears run a river
through the celestial abysm.
tomorrow charts a map
for a fusion of the schism.

like the dance of the dervish,
spectra spin "i" inside the lux
and no touch can numb us
from the fever of the flux.

along
the spine of
every shard of grass
sings a prayer
from the prairie
beckoning
the first
step
in
a
vast
stretch
of
miles

.

.

.

as time passes,
you will find
less and less
of a reason
to politicize
matters of the heart.

a simpler vocabulary will wish to
speak itself from your lips.

yes—
this jungle
is thronged with thorns…
but they cannot prick those
who move with the grace of air.

isotopic memories echo
high atop the dissonance,
only to avalanche along
the punctuated edges.

but beneath the rubble of nostalgia,
not all will remain in decay.
a time untouched by gravity
will resurrect a fertile chapter

of a new narrative
written in virgin hymns
yet to be bellowed,
yet to be hummed.

these are long and sad days—
where we droop about in a daze, finding none to help
but ourselves…
        when there is a whole world of those,
who suffer more deeply than we,
reaching for us to help lift them
to the heights of our low.

        sulking is a luxury that only few can afford.

a time will come
when the richness of our spirit
will measure more
than the wealth in our pockets.

a moment birthed just before death
when we all come to realize that
the celestial bounty that awaits us
is earned in what we gave away—
not in what we received.

those who demonize the world—
such a pity
for not seeing the demon within.
          they forget
the lens is also the mirror.

the very ones who try to destroy us
are the very ones to give us new life.
there is rebirth after death.
there is always light to be found in the dark.
there is an unwitting friend in every enemy.

and there is you amidst it all
living a story that is still yet to unfold.

the only crown i covet
is the one reserved
for those who have conquered the mind
which it is to sit upon.

the saddest part about our dreams
is that we love them so deeply,
but sometimes they do not love us back.
we can choose
to love them anyway.
to believe in them anyway.
to reach for them anyway.
the truth of one's heart does not need to be
reciprocated in order to exist.

often it is so,
that the very thing we desire
stands right before us–
so near, we can touch it
without the full extension of our arms.
and all that sits between
is the wall we built
to deprive ourselves from having it.

after day after day
of waiting for rain to come down
from imaginary clouds on sunny days,
i learned this the hard way:
living with joy is a choice.

the night will come.
but when the day is here,
there is still pleasure to be found
in its comforting warmth.

for when the sun sets,
those foils of laughter that escaped you
will find their way back to your breath.
it goes around...
it comes around...

        again
        and
        again...

a little boy fell in love with a butterfly whom he held close in the clasp of his hands. but more with each passing hour, she would applaud her limbs to encourage an escape to be free. while the boy was innocent, he was not unwise for he knew it was a crime to cage those with wings. so, he bowed before the great black willow, unfolded his praying hands, and worshipped upon a wish that she would be seduced to stay. but as she ascended into an echo of his eye, he breathed her a kiss with a sigh and said, "one day, i will grow tall until my chin can touch the sky and meet you on the clouds of what could have been."

we revive our future alive
when we rest our fears asleep,
dreaming our dreams
                so deeply
that we stir them into reality.

we are all birds in a cage with the latch unfastened.

this thing we do—
seeking out advice—
it is a mating ritual between the heart and the mind.
the gossiping of the subconscious with the conscious.
we already know what we are going to do
before we do it.
believe it. ask your own silence. she will tell you.
the next chapter was already written
before our entrance into the womb of this world.
                    and we are the authors.
                    and we have been here before.
                    and we will be here again
                              …if we want it.

there is no motherhood
which nurtures the child
but neglects the earth.
the fate of their future
is umbilical to the fate of the world.

loving eyes only see when dilated with foresight.

peering out into the wide horizon,
we search for something new.
signs and symbols seemingly surface
and we fancy it more a compass than a coincidence.
the quest continues for patterns in
> numbers,
>> colors,
>>> shapes,
>>>> and stars.
>>>> analyzing,
>>> decoding,
>> interpreting,
> calculating,
determining our next step's direction
by dissecting the words of others—
seeking permission to make manifest our flight.

> our light.

meanwhile, air quietly breathes through our lungs,
blood flows through our veins,
and joints bend with our bones just so—
forever drifting unplugged
like satellites of the living in this great unknown.

is this not magic?
does this not offer repose?
how can it not be clear enough for us to understand
that this life is our own to compose?

our dominion over the earth and its animals
decrees a duty for us to defend, not destroy,
the most vulnerable among us—
a power, if which betrayed,
can only result in our own demise.
there is no king without a kingdom.
there is no reign without the rise.

when we choose to survive
on what is tilled from the earth
and not on those who traverse it,
there are no tears to wipe away—
no need to plead for pardon—
because our bodies
will no longer decay as a grave
but proudly grow as a garden.

to all the young and wild at heart,
locked in cages without a key,
may we find a way to help
set each other free.

stand tall.
our spines were not designed for slouching.
we are embodiments of infinite potential,
bodies born to defy expectations,
a sunrise to a dying night,
a rogue tide to a splitting sea.
let the clouds spill around
your lack of obedience
to gravity's commands
that you should
sit down and play small.
stand tall.

there is no better leader
than the rhythm
from your own heart
giving your feet the pulse
by which to put one step
in front of the other
into the direction
of what you already know
is right for you.
everyone else—
everything else—
is just a drone of static
that makes it harder to hear
what needs to be done.

i surrendered to where a sea of shadows spanned infinity.
a million particles of light rained life between the synapses.
a vision of all that was and all that could ever be.
a view of all that was birth and all that was beauty.

just there beyond the bounds,
a baby bird in a wheat field
was learning to conquer the air,
crisscrossing in a circle
to the laced lines of infinity.

the heavens whispered,
"look up."
"i am everything you dreamed about laid out before you."

...and so, you see my love,
even though there is a schism between us
that we cannot seem to mend,
there is a blossom promised by the change of seasons—
as the tilt of the earth is certain to portend.

closer still we are forever to each other
than we are to all that surrounds,
for beneath the surface we drink from the same swallow—
entwined by the tangled roots from which we ground.

there
are a
    million
        beautifully
    simple
intricacies
to
the
    beating
    of
    a
    broken
        heart.

a crack in a glacial body
may leave two parts adrift,
but still they both sit
together afloat
on the
ocean.

so too it is the same with souls.

...and then somewhere along the way, you come across another. without warning. devoid of reason. carrying around the same weight of delusions that this road will actually lead to an intended destination. a soul that reminds you that you are alive, that breathing is magic, that magic is real, that there is still beauty to be found in the world, that this world is not real, that everything that came before was all just a playful ruse for you to be in the here and now – a now that passes faster than it was ever even here. soon it becomes clear. the clouds shift and your lips smirk as you come to remember that stars only shine in the night's sky. they are souls that ignite your soul all the brighter. a light that blinds you to surrender. a blissful paralysis of the minutiae and the mundanity. the sound of ten thousand silences colliding. a touch more familiar than the brush of your own hand against your skin. and when it happens, there is nothing more to do than to gaze softly into the abyss of their eyes, deep enough to find the place within them that will hear you as your heart beats "thank you".

a soul sleeps most sweetly when it has no stories left to hide. no fear remaining for the torrents surfed upon the traversing tide. from a heart that beats the red in surrender at the turn in the plot where it comes to realize that past's pain was to sail its way to future's beauty – a truth which those salted waters so seamlessly belied.

enlightenment comes at its own expense.
the sudden deluge of shadowed memories
of all that you ever did that was unjust
that you once defended as justified
drinks you in.
       it drowns

          you
          as it feeds itself to life.
               ...to light.
and the blissful chiaroscuro emerges in the horizon—
a distance tormented by the torrents
but made all the more inviting.

freedom dwells somewhere between the rhythm and the rhyme. it is the unapologetic disregard for the paradigm of time, where the difference between a laugh and a cry is none and the same like the cadence in a lion's roar untouched by a tame. it is the absence and forfeiture for the boundary of a line – this holy disobedience that i wholly claim as mine...

it is not so bad to be a crooked swing.
still it suspends itself in the air,
but never succumbs to the will of wind.

i am perched atop a grave in a cemetery of decaying dreams, and i cannot help but drift happily through the doldrums. in the cover of darkness and quiet, i am free to be what i was meant to be: spirited breath. and to dissolve in spaces meant for those much greater than i – it is its own kind of power. but still there burgeons a lonely despair inside of me. disappointment stymied by only more disappointment. and within the unsung bellow, i wallow. i take witness to the peculiar masochism in all the ways i tread through the currents of my own sorrow. and i remind myself that at a certain point, the earth has a way of making decisions for me. in these dark times, i wonder, perhaps the only light to be found is from the flame within...

to fall in love with another
who actually deserves your love–
now that is a star worth catching.

i would rather be mocked for caring too much than
accepted for caring too little. from the depth of my lungs,
i wish to respire all that my heart loves and in the way it
was intended to: unequivocally. unabashedly. ravishing
itself. this love is fire.

> it warms.
> it burns.
> it comforts as it destroys.
> it brings me to my knees as it breathes me alive.

> this hunt begins with the haunted.

some clouds never part
but the light finds a way to shine through them anyway.

this world is worth loving for.

the planets are spinning.
the stars are aligning.
the
angels
are
descending
mapping out exactly the journey
to take us from where we are
to where we need to be.
but all this is not as powerful as it may seem.
the earth needs to hear us howl
with every action,
with every choice,
with every thought,
with every pulse our hearts beat,
"this is what i want."

these passing winds
we call "woes"
move through us
to teach us
that we cannot be so easily blown

                over

and that still it is known
how to stand back

           up.

our lives are shadows cast before us
with each step into an imprint
of where we have already been.
traversing the transient,
one theatrical fiction at a time,
as we tread further and further
adrift on our voyage back to the sun.

we have descended
from where we will again
ascend.
this birth of flesh
is an illusion.
how can we be born
if we are always alive?
and what can it mean to grow older
if we never die?
this moment
is a well-intentioned lie
of maya's intoxication.

it
is
never
too
late
to
become
the
person
you
could
have
been

.

freezing rain fumbles
on the field of future's woes.
i breathe in deeply.

to see this world most clearly, one must close their eyes.

rooted in the soil,
i am seized in a seiza.
a frigid stillness—
severed only by the masticating winds.

ten toes crawl
into a burrow of the earth
and my palms search for solace
in the warmth of each other.

a single tear departs
into a freezing trail along my skin,
only to be greeted
by the vastness of the grayscape.

and my heart swells
steadfast with gratitude
that the change of seasons
is an eternal constant.

i elevate the frequency,
eclipsing the flame,
to the lotus of a thousand petals
and i see you
in
every
chasm
of
black
behind
the
curtain
of
my
eyes

.

the greatest strength
lay not in the brutal predator,
nor in the stoic prey,
but in the humble planarian
who multiplies when divided.

what we seek lies just below the depth of our breath.
dive in.

on this road,

we lay waste to ourselves
in hammering at walls
that are already far behind

us.

there is an ember
in every pile of ash.
fan that flame
and another fire will arise.
every end
is the beginning
of something new.

hate.
devours.
itself.
it is a single-toothed beast
that clumsily preys upon its own tongue.
ignore the roar.
it has not the claws to climb the mountain before you
and its ascent to the better you still to come.

it was a posthumous delusion,
as blissful a dream as it may be,
to think that we could ever recapture
what has been denied to us by destiny.

if you offer your hand
to lift up a man
hanging from the edge,
be sure he does not fall
away with your arm.
martyrdom serves no master.

to listen twice as much
as one speaks
is to one day
be able to say something worth listening to.

the final moments of us
finished like a fermata
as the last note
in the last measure
of a short but soaring song—
        the kind
        you rewind
        soon after the closing chord
        has been strummed.

astral planes can emerge
in the throes of those
where copper thuds
against hapless hands.

and such swift benevolence
can seamlessly deliver one into
a rapture of repose where
celestial bodies naughtily collide

with sanguine dreams.

i fell forward into the cosmos
and drowned myself
into the deluge of the abyss.
it was only there
that i found the air–
          the pulse–
          the rhythm–
          the color–
all that was never false–
rescued by the pull of me
to the under.

paralyzed
we are with the problems of the past
that were only conceived because
we then too were not
present in the present.
but if we are to look back,
then let us look to the beginning.
nevermore pure were we
than at birth,
and perhaps it is in that moment
where our mind should reside.

we cannot quench the thirst of a dying man with our tears
any more than we can feed him with our prayers.

i will never arrive at my destination,
this i know.
but in this pursuit of perfection,
i am alive.

hidden within our third eye
lays the answer to every question,
the calm to every storm,
and the light to its own darkness.

break through.
let go.
fall in.

from the collision comes the escape.

a swallow of the summer's air sits heavy on my tongue.
smelled and felt but never seen, as it snows from the sun.
alone i stand but i sense the others.
this swell of light is too bright to imagine.
a viscid mist descends and from another life i remember:
souls are clandestine.

at the turn of the datura's nocturnal bloom,
upon the midnight's slumber,
i glissade across the sleeping blades
where twigs and twine contort asunder.

the stubborn spiders who wed thy web,
pendulous to their silver cord,
trickle down on a single thread—
a greeting soft, but not unheard.

even at this moonlit hour,
this blackened air can still be sweet.
pond lilies throned upon the tepid water,
and still a place to dip my feet.

enamored by the clamor
from the chorus of the cricket,
i found somewhere to lose myself
in the thick of this thicket.

❖

the earth blooms
from both the sun and the rain
just as we do.

dreams of tomorrow
destroy today.
let us not delay any longer.
the whole world is laid out before us,
our veins are raging with purpose,
and these moments are to be set ablaze.

now is right now.

begin.

to live a life of luster,
we must learn how to love.
that is to say,
we must unlearn all of the ways
the world has taught us not to.

it is opaque–
the window through which we see the future that lies ahead.
it is here,
a trilling dawn to turn the page on a story unread.
it is true,
a mistake can morph into a cavity of apathy.
it is you–
an angel to smile down and fray away my frailty.

the irony of you is that as we fall in love,
i feel as if i have found everything in this world
i could ever want.
and yet, together as we hold hands,
even more is possible still.

was it happenstance,
that curious trice,
where i found myself
in the same space as you?

i could feel the fears you were fleeing from,
taste the divine upon your tongue,
hear the wild that ran within,
and in this voyage of clairvoyance,
see that none was safe from sin.

i want to meet you for the first time

again.

the
height
of
one's
flight
is
foretold
at
the
seat
of
one's
feet.
the story of our journey begins here.

the most peaceful slumber of night there ever was,
was the one earned by the ownership of the day.
run against the setting of the sun,
and you will revel in the moon.

this is all a gift,
from what i have come to see.
a wide horizon
of miles to travel,
of fruit to pick
from fertile trees,
of tears to be shed
on thirsty loam
to give birth to a space
where we can heal our weary feet,
of screams to share unheard
so the sweet of silence can prevail.
apparitions of the past.
angels of the present.
aspirations of the future.
they all dance past me in a radiating bolero.

fortune does not favor the fearful,
nor hold firm to the path of the bold,
but goes the way of the giddy.
this you are certain to see.

look closely.

sprawled across the grass
with an ear against the earth
as feathered clouds sauntered by
alongside the hallowed meniscus,
gravid loam parted
for the daze to take root
and croon its ethereal lullaby.

what the world needs most
is for children to grow up
in that whimsical way
where they do not.

show your wounds.
let others see them
bleed and bruise,
blister and boil.
so that when they heal,
others will know
that their wounds will
one day heal too.

climb a knotted willow tree
on an otiose sunday afternoon
and unfurl your eyes toward the catkin.
as you dangle askew from the back of your knees,
you will start to see things much differently.

when the sky goes dark
and the rains fall heavy upon your shoulders,
remember that even the soil must split
for a seed to sprout.

in that darkest hour of the night,
it may seem that everything begins
to take the shape of stones—
in situ silhouettes of the faint.
move through them as the mist—
an apparition of the ubiquitous.
and let the marvels of the moon
shimmer from the dew
you leave upon their rounds.

when you come upon a squirming worm
drying in the sun,
rescue him to the grass
and rollick in the field together
as your souls become one.

in these twisted woods,
the journey before us is not the path itself,
but to walk without breaking a branch,
to be heard without making a sound,
and to strive for remembrance
while still revering all that surrounds.

sometimes,
just before i fall asleep
and float away into a lull of reverie,
i have a moment
where i can remember
what it felt like to be a boy.

it is the dream before the dream.

tilt
    your
        head
and think of something strange.
                this is how magic happens.

unflinchingly,
i bullied my motherless wound
where hemoglobin drip drops
blotted the concrete
beneath my sullied shoes.

"it was a good day,"
i mused with a grin,
for i knew not how it came to be
with so many antics
from which to choose.

we pass through this life like the wind.
always coming.
forever going.
never here,
but everywhere.
there is no adieu for the air.

born in water,
we breathe.
grown to walk,
we falter.
no wings,
but meant to fly.

these seas
are brimming with passengers
sinking on punctured ships,
seeking neither an anchor
nor an oar,
and not one of them has saved a seat for you.

give them not even a moment more of survival
with the float of your tears.
you are blessed to be swimming alone
against the waves,
along the crest,
for only you will make it back to the sands.

these bones
holding me together–
i can feel them growing older.
i am less able to run now,
but so much more able
to stand firm.

in a world corroding in anger,
polluted with apathy,
stirring with ignorance,
and drowning in vanity,

be the silence that only love can allay.
still the mind with reverence for another.
be a mountain peeking through the mist of clouds.

this i remind. this i must remember.

have no jealousy
for what others appear to be
or the façade they display for us to see.
inside all hearts,
there plays the drama of a silent tragedy—
just as there is with you and me.

be soft
with those who are not so good with goodbyes.
it may not be that they do not care.
it may be that they care so much
that they want to leave a part of themselves
with you before they go.
but they know, deep within,
that the more of this life they live through
and the more partings they make peace with,
the greater the chance they might just give away
the one piece that collapses them into their own
u   n   r   a   v   e   l .

you are more beautiful than your mirror will admit—
even more than it can understand.

right now,
in this very moment,
you are but one choice away
from changing everything that ever was
into everything that could ever be.
it is all just a matter of
letting go and grabbing on
at the same time.

...like a child on a swing.
        ...like the swordplay of a king.

there is meaning in the melancholy—
much more than in the blissful continuum
of sunny days and estranged sorrows.
from its purpose comes the path—
our way out…
and on the other side, we will be greeted by the night's orb
who was patiently awaiting our arrival.
there, just above the crescent, the blackbirds sing a song,
"it is okay to want to cry.

        it is okay to want to hold these tears back.

            it is okay to fail in doing so."

when we look at the world in which we live
and at the crevices of our own mind,
we find a depth of darkness so profound
that only love can illuminate.

some things in life are best left to be felt than to be understood. cleverness has led us astray to the disarray of this world, and perhaps it is time that we create a new one. an abysm of dark spaces that are illumined by the goodness of our spirit, and not further blackened by the guilefulness of our reason. a union of fields with humble warriors marching to the sound of their own beating hearts. a terrestrial body where its limbs work to alleviate the plight of others, rather than worship for passage through the palatial gates of a purported heaven. a labyrinth of journeys explored by brave wanderers who proudly announce their stumbles through the echoes of swinging trees and mounting seas, so that those who have not yet embarked upon the path may have a calmer storm before them. under a certainty of death, the rain will one day extinguish our flame. but there is no such promise that we are to fully live while being alive. these reigns are ours alone to hold. let us not squander the remainder of our time lamenting tears of false squalor and showering the sky with our hollow wishes. let us revere the rivers from which we drink, the soil from where we stand, and surrender before the crashing skies of this wild enigma with the thunder of purpose beating through our veins. let us feed our fill on the divine privilege to be alive and quench our tongues with the light pouring down from the rays of our forgiving sun. here and now, we can choose to forgive our follies, forget our foes, and forge ahead with the fortitude to defy all that gravity has for us to endure – forfeiting the myriad of justifications for why we continue as we are and remerging allegiant to the pursuit of becoming better than we have ever been. in this quiet unknowing, we must honor the magic inside ourselves and begin to perform miracles for each other. with our hands and hearts as one, may we bow before this magnificent horizon of possibilities and kneel down to kiss the earth.

these words spiraling upon the pillowed pond
are the pulsating ripples from a heart
that finally learned how to love.

K

I

S

S

S

T

H

E

E

A

R

T

H